Be Strong. Be Brave. Be Humble.

Be Badass Every Day.

A JOURNAL

ROGENA MITCHELL-JONES JOURNALS

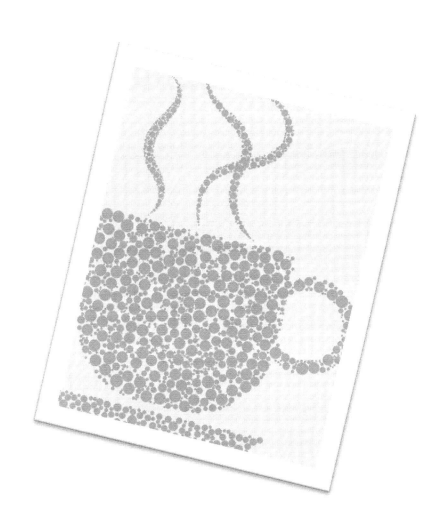

Be Strong. Be Brave. Be Humble. Be Badass.

Be Strong. Be Brave. Be Humble. Be Badass.

Be Strong. Be Brave. Be Humble. Be Badass.

Be Strong. Be Brave. Be Humble. Be Badass.

Be Strong. Be Brave. Be Humble. Be Badass.

Be Strong. Be Brave. Be Humble. Be Badass.

Be Strong. Be Brave. Be Humble. Be Badass.

Be Strong. Be Brave. Be Humble. Be Badass.

Be Strong. Be Brave. Be Humble. Be Badass.

Be Strong. Be Brave. Be Humble. Be Badass.

Be Strong. Be Brave. Be Humble. Be Badass.

Be Strong. Be Brave. Be Humble. Be Badass.

Be Strong. Be Brave. Be Humble. Be Badass.

Be Strong. Be Brave. Be Humble. Be Badass.

Be Strong. Be Brave. Be Humble. Be Badass.

Be Strong. Be Brave. Be Humble. Be Badass.

Be Strong. Be Brave. Be Humble. Be Badass.

Be Strong. Be Brave. Be Humble. Be Badass.

Be Strong. Be Brave. Be Humble. Be Badass.

Be Strong. Be Brave. Be Humble. Be Badass.

Be Strong. Be Brave. Be Humble. Be Badass.

Be Strong. Be Brave. Be Humble. Be Badass.

Be Strong. Be Brave. Be Humble. Be Badass.

Be Strong. Be Brave. Be Humble. Be Badass.

Be Strong. Be Brave. Be Humble. Be Badass.

Be Strong. Be Brave. Be Humble. Be Badass.

Be Strong. Be Brave. Be Humble. Be Badass.

Be Strong. Be Brave. Be Humble. Be Badass.

Be Strong. Be Brave. Be Humble. Be Badass.

Be Strong. Be Brave. Be Humble. Be Badass.

Be Strong. Be Brave. Be Humble. Be Badass.

Be Strong. Be Brave. Be Humble. Be Badass.

Be Strong. Be Brave. Be Humble. Be Badass.

Be Strong. Be Brave. Be Humble. Be Badass.

Be Strong. Be Brave. Be Humble. Be Badass.

Be Strong. Be Brave. Be Humble. Be Badass.

Be Strong. Be Brave. Be Humble. Be Badass.

Be Strong. Be Brave. Be Humble. Be Badass.

Be Strong. Be Brave. Be Humble. Be Badass.

Be Strong. Be Brave. Be Humble. Be Badass.

Be Strong. Be Brave. Be Humble. Be Badass.

Be Strong. Be Brave. Be Humble. Be Badass.

Be Strong. Be Brave. Be Humble. Be Badass.

Be Strong. Be Brave. Be Humble. Be Badass.

Be Strong. Be Brave. Be Humble. Be Badass.

Be Strong. Be Brave. Be Humble. Be Badass.

Be Strong. Be Brave. Be Humble. Be Badass.

Be Strong. Be Brave. Be Humble. Be Badass.

Be Strong. Be Brave. Be Humble. Be Badass.

Be Strong. Be Brave. Be Humble. Be Badass.

Be Strong. Be Brave. Be Humble. Be Badass.

Be Strong. Be Brave. Be Humble. Be Badass.

Be Strong. Be Brave. Be Humble. Be Badass.

Be Strong. Be Brave. Be Humble. Be Badass.

Be Strong. Be Brave. Be Humble. Be Badass.

Be Strong. Be Brave. Be Humble. Be Badass.

Be Strong. Be Brave. Be Humble. Be Badass.

Be Strong. Be Brave. Be Humble. Be Badass.

Be Strong. Be Brave. Be Humble. Be Badass.

Be Strong. Be Brave. Be Humble. Be Badass.

Be Strong. Be Brave. Be Humble. Be Badass.

Be Strong. Be Brave. Be Humble. Be Badass.

Be Strong. Be Brave. Be Humble. Be Badass.

Be Strong. Be Brave. Be Humble. Be Badass.

Be Strong. Be Brave. Be Humble. Be Badass.

Be Strong. Be Brave. Be Humble. Be Badass.

Be Strong. Be Brave. Be Humble. Be Badass.

Be Strong. Be Brave. Be Humble. Be Badass.

Be Strong. Be Brave. Be Humble. Be Badass.

Be Strong. Be Brave. Be Humble. Be Badass.

Be Strong. Be Brave. Be Humble. Be Badass.

Be Strong. Be Brave. Be Humble. Be Badass.

Be Strong. Be Brave. Be Humble. Be Badass.

Be Strong. Be Brave. Be Humble. Be Badass.

Be Strong. Be Brave. Be Humble. Be Badass.

Be Strong. Be Brave. Be Humble. Be Badass.

Be Strong. Be Brave. Be Humble. Be Badass.

Be Strong. Be Brave. Be Humble. Be Badass.

Be Strong. Be Brave. Be Humble. Be Badass.

Be Strong. Be Brave. Be Humble. Be Badass.

Be Strong. Be Brave. Be Humble. Be Badass.

Be Strong. Be Brave. Be Humble. Be Badass.

Be Strong. Be Brave. Be Humble. Be Badass.

Be Strong. Be Brave. Be Humble. Be Badass.

Be Strong. Be Brave. Be Humble. Be Badass.

Be Strong. Be Brave. Be Humble. Be Badass.

TO ORDER ADDITIONAL JOURNALS, GO TO
AMAZON OR THE CREATESPACE ONLINE STORE.
SEARCH ROGENA MITCHELL-JONES JOURNALS.

OR DIRECT FROM THE AUTHOR AT
ROGENA@ROGENAMITCHELL.COM

ROGENA MITCHELL-JONES MANUSCRIPT SERVICE
WWW.ROGENAMITCHELL.COM

"Having worked as a screenwriter for 31 years, I was worn out by countless battles with clueless development execs who wanted to weigh in on how to 'fix' my screenplays, so I was nervous about hiring an 'editor' to help me refine my first novel. It was my experience that those who could actually write, wrote; those who couldn't write, edited. Rogena changed all that. Frankly, I wouldn't publish a thing without her.

"She was forceful with her criticisms without being intractable. She was collaborative without being pedantic, and most importantly, she took the time to analyze, understand and respect my unique style without trying to impose her own. She's an ace with punctuation, something we ignore in screenwriting, and she's a wiz at formatting, making the "e" in e-book stand for 'easy.'

"I am deeply indebted to her and remain one of her biggest fans. Honestly, if there's anything in my book you don't like, I'd bet real money that it's an instance where I ignored Rogena's advice. That's how good she is."

Kevin Alyn Elders is an Author, Screenwriter, Producer, and Director. From his early works, including the Iron Eagle action adventure series, through his later works, including Echelon Conspiracy, he has sold 23 out of 26 original screenplays and has written in many genres for notable directors, actors and producers such as Oliver Stone, Sean Connery, Sylvester Stallone, Arnold Schwarzenegger, Joel Silver, Albert S. Ruddy, and Louis Gossett Jr. His taut, compelling, suspense-filled narratives have found their latest incarnation in his upcoming Screen Novel Series of Paperbacks, EBooks, and Audiobooks. www.kevinalynelders.com.

* * * * *

"On the shore, there was a voice of reason. It was a voice who spoke of telling a story, not about gerunds and gerundives. It spoke of the power of words strung together, not only to convey a concept, but also to tell a story, to draw forth from the reader their untold, unrealized story. And the voice was Rogena Mitchell-Jones."

Baer Charlton, Author of the Pulitzer Prize Nominated book, Stoneheart: A Path of Identity and Redemption

Rogena Mitchell-Jones Manuscript Service

A Professional Editing Service | Freelance Editing with Affordable Rates
Striving for Excellence for You, the Author, Providing Concise Literary & Technical Editing.

"MY NAME IS ROGENA, AND I AM A BOOKAHOLIC."

THE FIRST STEP IS ADMISSION, RIGHT? OK, SERIOUSLY.

Currently, Rogena Mitchell-Jones lives in South Jersey with her wife, Karen, and their extremely pampered cats. If she isn't at home editing or reading, you might find her on the beach—book in hand.

Her background consists of over 25 years in journalism and now editing full time for independent authors internationally since 2013. Her clientele base includes a vast array of Amazon, USA Today, and NY Times Best Selling Authors.

The end of 2014, Rogena was nominated as best editor in an awards event sponsored by The Kindle Hub—TKH Book Awards 2014. With nearly sixty editors competing, she advanced to the finals and came in second in the final competition. With the title of BEST EDITOR 2014 Finalist, it shows hard work does pay off.

She isn't a writer—She's an editor. She is here because she wants to assist you, the author, in creating a manuscript free of typographical errors, including misspelled words, grammatical errors, and inconsistencies in plot and characters.

She gives attention to detail. With this attention to detail, she is able to polish your future best seller, like polishing fine silver that once belonged to your grandmother. Let's make your manuscript the masterpiece you have dreamed of publishing.

She is an editor, not an author. She is a reader, not a writer. She is a Copy Editor. She wants to live in your story while reading your manuscript.

She is here to assist you so you will have a result allowing your future readers to enjoy your published work.

Contact her on Facebook or via email at rogena@rogenamitchell.com.

ROGENA MITCHELL-JONES MANUSCRIPT SERVICE
WWW.ROGENAMITCHELL.COM

61376739R00057

Made in the USA
Lexington, KY
08 March 2017